Create Your Life's Masterpiece

Simple Secrets to
Winning the Money Game
that Anyone Can Use
to Build an Extraordinary Life

Wendy Yau Sum Cheung

ISBN-13: 978-1-7328719-1-5

ISBN-10: 1-7328719-1-4

Published by: Celebrity Expert Author

http://celebrityexpertauthor.com

Canadian Address:	US Address:
1108 - 1155 The High Street,	1300 Boblett Street
Coquitlam, BC, Canada	Unit A-218
V3B.7W4	Blaine, WA 98230
Phone: (604) 941-3041	Phone: (866) 492-6623
Fax: (604) 944-7993	Fax: (250) 493-6603

Contents

Overture:
My Composition For You

The Best Way to Predict Your Future is to Create It.
Abraham Lincoln

HOW DOES ONE predict one's future? Abraham Lincoln says, "The best way to predict your future is to create it." I agree. I believe in creating our future and this is why I want to write this book — to help you create your future by creating your life's masterpiece. I hope to empower and inspire you to take actions that will ultimately bring about positive impact in your life, especially for those of you who have an innermost passion or a long lost dream.

As time is precious, I will delve right to the heart of making your life extraordinary by opening your eyes to the possibilities of achieving what you want while enjoying the comfort of knowing that your finances are in order.

I congratulate those of you who have achieved what you want by allowing me to be involved in your financial life. I am glad you are enjoying the comfort of knowing your finances are in order because of the bold decisions you have made since the start! Whether you bought this book or were given one as a gift, I hope reading it will encourage you to keep creating for your future's sake and to continue reminding yourself to keep paying it forward by helping others.

Avery, our only son, your daddy and I hope to leave this book as a legacy of our love for you and all your children to come. I hope all future generations will benefit from reading it as well; it is part of me that I can leave behind as a practical gift.

A warmest hello to those of you who just picked this book up in the hope of learning how to create your life's masterpiece. I aim to inspire and motivate you so that when you are at the last page, you will have discovered how to begin achieving financial freedom by using my proven strategies and by applying my successful business and life's principles.

Movement I:
Making Money to Change Your Lifestyle

MANY OF US have hidden interests or childhood dreams which we have placed aside for obvious pragmatic reasons as life does happen on a daily basis. We grow up, get a job, get married, have a family, and then go to work to provide for the family. But, for some of us, there is that longing to pursue a certain dream or to go where that once-upon-a-time passion is. Do you still remember your answer to the question, "What do you want to be when you grow up?" Are you in touch with your actual passion or even have time to think about it? What is stopping or preventing you from living a life that supports your pursuit of those interests or passions on a daily basis?

Whenever I ask that last question, I generally get a variety of responses but they all boil down to one thing: **money!**

Of course, all of us need money to survive. We need money to buy food, clothes and shoes, pay bills, support our parents and provide for our children. But how about beyond that? How about happiness? Some of you may be happy with just surviving, but how about those of you who are not? You may, like me, want more to life than just surviving with the burning desire to live beyond that. But I learnt that money alone does not buy real happiness. I firmly believe that it can be used to create opportunities for enjoyable experiences to bring meaningful memories for oneself. That is what I mean by **creating your life's masterpiece**, and that is what I hope to help you do.

Undoubtedly, the lack of money prevents us from living a life. But most times, our inner fears, self-doubts, inescapable obligations and unexpected factors get in our ways. That is when you need courage to do something about it to bring yourself out of the current situation to a place of freedom. That is when you have to honor your innermost passion and go for it. Believe that you are capable in creating a viable plan for yourself to diligently follow and make it happen. Only then you will move towards living a happier and a more purposeful life.

Let me start by talking about the effects of money under the five categories of people's lifestyle in terms of financial levels:

The Five S'es of Financial Levels Affecting Lifestyle

1. Survival Level

We all started out creating financial independence by making sure there is food to eat, clothes to wear and a roof over our head. These are basic human needs.

2. Security Level

Once we are able to merely survive, we want to ensure the quality of tomorrow will be just as good as today. We should not have to worry if we can afford our next meal or our next month's rent. This level is above the survival mode, but it carries some uncertainties beyond the time frame of six months to a year.

3. Stability Level

People who are in this level are confident of their chosen career path. They know that there is room for growth in the future and they are certainly able to imagine retirement someday. This level generally would entail home ownership. However, the picture of the future is heavily depended upon their current income and status quo situations.

4. Success Level

When we know we can comfortably take care of our family, we strive to raise our standard of living. This means taking our kids to private school, vacation several times a year, splurges on celebrations and nice dinners out with our loved ones. At this level, we have the habit of increasing our spending, the desire for a more luxurious lifestyle and the confidence to creating this wealth.

5. Significance Level

When all of our needs and wants are mostly met, we begin the endeavour to make a difference in this world, searching for the meaning of life and trying to find significance. We are either engrossed with our hobbies, traveling to interesting places, involved with charities or inclined to help others who are less fortunate. People in this category look for a variety of experiences such as continuous personal growth, leaving a lasting legacy or pursuing a worthwhile cause to contribute to.

Since money affects our lifestyle everyday, we have to learn how to make money so that we can move from one level to another level with the aim of arriving at the highest level where financial freedom is achieved.

Everyone trades a product or a service to receive money. For instance, an accountant charges by the hour while a plumber charges by the job for providing a service. In another instance, by selling a product, a salesperson earns commissions while a corporate employee earns a salary with potential bonuses. Every one of us grows up with the concept of earning money by exchanging something, but I have discovered that **the power of money extends way beyond a trade for time or a product.** Just straight trading would take years and years if I want to earn millions of dollars, and that is definitely not efficient at all. This is the lesson that I quickly learned as a business owner.

I started Mozart School of Music right out of university. I decided that I wanted a business that would fund my lifestyle while pursuing a career in songwriting. As a business owner, all of my time was taken up in running the school and teaching my students. Therefore, there was no time left for me to freely follow my passion to be a songwriter. I quickly realized that in order to earn the amount of income I want from this music business, it would require giving up a lot of myself. I would have to work non-stop, and years would pass before I could reach my goal of writing a song that would hit the billboard charts. So, I began looking at other options. **I explored financial concepts and it led me to real estate.**

The reason I took an interest in this field was primarily due to the probability of success stories around creating wealth using this vehicle as opposed to other options. **"90% of all millionaires become so by owning real estate" as quoted by Andrew Carnegie.** Therefore, I figured, my odds would be pretty high in excelling in this field because there is already an established infrastructure for wealth-building.

Purchasing rental properties has been the traditional way of creating income passively. Many people I know became financially successful by just choosing to purchase rental properties and by just applying some common sense. In 2008, immediately after attending a real estate seminar organized by the Real Estate Investment Network, I decided to go one hundred percent full-on with this mindset of creating income through real estate. I started Peak Performance Investment Limited with a few business partners, and within a very short period of time, the company became a phenomenal success. It has purchased more than one hundred houses by raising capital among many investors who appreciate the turnkey system we have developed. The turnkey system is a step-by step way of taking care of our clients: acquisition, financing, insurance, legality and property management, making sure that every single property in our portfolio produces a strong cash flow plus a high potential for value appreciation in Greater Vancouver, Fraser Valley, Northern British Columbia and Alberta.

Following this success, we founded Alture Properties Incorporation in 2009 to create for our clients the option of using their Tax-Free Savings Account, Registered Education Savings Plan and Registered Retired Savings Plan to invest in fully managed hard assets with added tax benefits. This option is super attractive as it makes it much easier for investors to get involved in the real estate market without having to take on mortgage payments and handling property management duties. Alture took care of the whole condo conversion process: interior renovations, tenant management, bookkeeping and even educating our clients on how to take advantage of the current market.

From 2009 to present, Alture has been involved in land developments by designing master plans for multi-family communities encompassing commercial buildings, high-rise condos and wood frame low-rise residences. Alture has successfully developed projects in British Columbia, Toronto and Alberta where the market value of these developments is often well over one hundred million dollars. Alture is continuously growing and thriving, and you can find it on the Toronto Stock Exchange (Private Market).

This success of my companies gave me the money and the time to pursue my passion for songwriting. In 2013, I co-produced my first album entitled "The Color of Love" and several of the songs on that album hit the Hong Kong Billboard Chart with "Homeless but Not Hopeless" and "Cherish Every Minute" winning

Metro Radio Hits Music Award for Composition. As I was invited to the Gala to receive my awards, this was the realization of one of my dreams of walking on the red carpet and meeting many celebrities. This was no longer me predicting my future, but me creating my future by **creating my life's masterpiece.**

Movement II:
The Eight Strategies of Profiting off the Real Estate Market

I HAVE MADE my money by profiting in the real estate world and so can you. The means for you to do this as well may be categorized into one or more of the following 8 strategies:

Strategy #1. Buy and Hold - This is the simplest method. All you have to do is purchase a property in a desirable area and rent it out to good tenants. To find good tenants, it is very necessary that you do a full credit check and make several reference calls to previous landlords. If this task is not in your calling, you can delegate it to a trusted property management firm. Typically, the firm finds new tenants, collects rents, does house visits and provides many other related services for a percentage of all rents collected, plus fees for acquiring new tenants or handling renovations, You can maximize the benefit of using this Buy and Hold method by purchasing a multi-unit property, such as a duplex, a fourplex or an apartment building to give you a regular stream of residual cash flow through inflation protected rental income. This continues while holding this property until, either the mortgage is paid off resulting in an increased net income stream for retirement, the market value has increased enabling the option to sell at that higher price for profit or the time comes to pass your property onto the next generation as an inheritance. As you can see, Buy and Hold can be a great retirement strategy.

Strategy #2. Buy and Flip - This strategy calls for perfect market timing and risk tolerance plus some aptitude in the renovation department. It is most suitable for a handyman or someone who enjoys putting in the sweat equity in a project. The typical downfall is underestimating costs and the time frame to finish the project, while overestimating selling price. If this is what you intend to do, make sure to hire a professional realtor to assist on evaluating selling price. To ensure you do make money or the most money, start off by watching out on the buy side — the steeper the discount, the more risk protected you will be. A smart way is to get quotes from multiple contractors prior to purchasing your property in order to establish that your budget is within reason. In addition, to be on the safe side, I strongly advise you to add a reasonable buffer to the highest quote. Remember to factor in selling costs (realtor fees), legal fees, financing interests and your time as a renovator. Renovating a house for profit requires a much more complicated approach than renovating your house or your kitchen for yourself. The key to the success of this strategy is to find the **right match** for the type of renovation to the target audience you are aiming to sell to. This is very tricky, and therefore, my advice to you is to do some research by visiting other renovated properties in the marketplace, and to discuss your plans with your realtor. Be mindful of keeping the project on track by drafting up a pro-forma work schedule and a timeline in advance.

Strategy #3. Buy and Subdivide - This is what developers do to make very lucrative money. If you already have a piece of land or intend to purchase one, make sure you check with city hall on all the regulatory guidelines for your intention to develop. Subdivision takes time and effort because the process to applying for an approval can take a very long time and so buying a piece of land for future potential value will end up putting the purchaser at an unnecessary risk of losing money instead. It is reasonable for you to pay a little more for a piece of land, but you do have to **think twice** before overexposing yourself to risks by holding onto something that depends on the market or regulatory body to make your profit. Added to that risk of losing money is the funds needed to pay for the costs of holding on to that property. Unexpected market changes or city requirements for adherence can throw you off your original timeline. Therefore, **be prepared** for such contingencies, and make sure you have enough cash to pay for the mortgage, property taxes, insurance and related soft costs (architectural, engineering, financial, pre and post-construction) to successfully finish this project.

Strategy #4. Buy and Convert - Condo conversion is a strategy that our company used to make our first million for our investors. Even more incredible is that we were able to obtain this profit prior to completing the project by using skip transfers (an innovative method to raise funds to pay for the purchase of the original building prior to owning the building) and staggered closing. What we did was that we secured a multi-family apartment building in Edmonton, Alberta, and negotiated with the seller to allow access for renovations and legal conversion before our actual completion date, and because we had built an incredible show room, we were able to sell off all the unit entitlements to investors before the renovation process even began. I was so proud of my team because of their stellar coordination skills. We could not have pulled this off successfully without trusted team players and a group of very organized renovators. The entire renovation took a full year to complete with a great deal of tenancy logistics to maneuver. So, for you to use this strategy, make very sure you have an **experienced team of people** who can work for you with the **endgame** in mind.

Strategy #5. Buy and Resell - Purchasing a pre-sale (a property before it is built) or an existing property that you want to speculate on because you think it will have an increase in value over a short period of time has been the most common way of making money in the real estate market. If the area of your choice has **obvious signs** of near future infrastructural changes such as a highway expansion, new Skytrain stations, subway stations, light rail transit, re-gentrification or improved density by other developers, then look into jumping on the bandwagon **before the changes happen**. Furthermore, in making your final decisions, also factor in reputable top-rated schools, community centres and close access to shopping hubs. All of these elements will provide better economic protection during a sudden downturn in the market, especially at a time when you want or have to liquidate. We all know that if there is no buyer, there is no market. My golden rule is never, I repeat, NEVER ever put yourself in a situation where you are forced to sell a property at any cost. Just follow the direction people are taking. Go where they go and do what they do to purchase a property with the highest probability of selling it for a profit, even in a soft market. (A soft market is a time when there are more sellers than buyers.)

Strategy #6. Buy and Build - Building a home for profit may be something you can do on the side during your spare time or full on as a serious business. Whether you are in it on the side or full on, **building** a house for yourself and then **selling** at some point in time is **creating equity**. The most important point for you to understand is that the house you reside in is not considered to be an asset unless it has rental suites. Without rental suites, it is actually a liability to you because it costs money to maintain it. If you have not chosen being a builder as your career choice, you should hire one to build you the house, and then you can sell it to profit from the cost of the house and the cost of the construction. But you must be very cautious and choose your builder carefully. In addition to that, you must ensure you have enough cash reserves and/or construction financing. Throughout the process, you must watch out for cost overruns, unrealistic project timelines and volatile market conditions. During an upswing, this method would be a perfect home run, but during a downturn, it requires patience and a good sense of timing which means you need to hold on to the property by living in it or renting it out until it is time to put it back into the market again. Regardless of whether you are choosing to live in it or rent out, there is the possibility of you drawing out the equity to kickoff your next investment on another rental property.

Strategy #7. Buy and Operate - This strategy is my favorite because of my entrepreneurial nature. Buying a commercial space and using it to run a business is a formula that works well for business owners who are not fond of leasing space for a long haul and whose ultimate goal is to **own the place in which they operate, thus making it their asset**. This makes perfect sense to me. You see, when you pay a monthly lease, you are helping the landlord pay off his or her mortgage. So, why not keep the equity part of the mortgage to your own business and also reap the rewards of future appreciation? This means instead of paying monthly leases, you are paying monthly mortgages. This is the very essence of building equity for the business operating in it, and owning the opportunity of selling it later when there is profit to be made. Another best outcome is the peace of mind you get in knowing your business will not be threatened by regular increases in the rental rate or the chance of having to relocate due to the landlord's change of heart. Consequently, when the business excels, it produces another stream of wealth-building opportunities which you might otherwise not have if the operating venue is not an asset. Overall, I truly love this strategy and consider it to be the best here.

Strategy #8. Buy and Develop - This is the most complicated strategy and it places you under another category of real estate investments. It requires you to **form a full-time real estate team who can dedicate their time, knowledge and resources to bring your vision into concrete reality.** Whether the land you want to buy is for developing multi-family housing or commercial buildings (retail/office/industrial) or for a mixed-use development site, it is critical to consult with a project manager who has much experience in rolling out projects from inception to completion. The presence of due diligence on the site is imperative. And the dedication to carry out environmental and feasibility studies, write up appraisal reports and work in person with the city planner is a must if you want to take advantage of the existing community infrastructure or if you want to improve it. Along the way are many possible surprises that require a change in conceptual plans, construction processes, sales schedules, marketing timelines and financing options which may steeply cut into your bottom line. These are all the risk variables one would have to consider when becoming a real estate developer. Raising capital to fund such projects requires a dedicated sales team, but the entire process comes with many legal ramifications, and therefore, legal fees and up-front consultation cost can be substantial. Before jumping in with eyes closed, it is very necessary for you to take a very good look at all the pros and cons of such a strategy while carefully weighing all the options presented at the financial level you are at. Once your realistic scope of abilities and financial boundaries has been diligently determined to be in your favour, only then you should decide to proceed to draw up a solid business plan by consulting with an experienced mentor in this area.

These eight strategies are ways to help you make money and move up the financial level to where you find financial freedom. You can pick one strategy or a few strategies that are best suited for you and be consistent in studying, creating, implementing and executing your plan with the aim of reaching your financial goals in a timely manner. Time factor is a reality in any business venture, and it is certainly a factor in getting into the real estate market, whether you are using one strategy or a combination of strategies..

My company Alture Properties, employed Strategy #8 (Buy and Develop). Initially, it took two years for our business goal to come to fruition because we had to wait to be given the status that allows us to legally receive RRSP, RESP and TFSA subscriptions from the public. But we wasted no time at all because during that waiting period, we utilized Strategy #4 (Buy and Convert) to gain experience in condo conversions by working with other developers. This combination of strategies helped moved us up very quickly from our initial financial position to a much higher level. Prior to launching into developments, we already owned and managed a portfolio of many assets. This success is the result of much discipline, laser beam focus and firm determination. We did not settle for less. We kept working conscientiously to make money to witness success. The key was to maintain focus, and to have no fear of failure to get in our way. We had a clear goal and we zeroed in on our target. When you work diligently and keep pursuing what you want, you will get to the financial level you are aiming for.

When you make the money needed for the kind of lifestyle you seek, you are creating your life's masterpiece. That is the future I want to see you create.

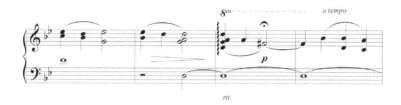

Movement III:
Three General Approaches to Investing in Real Estate

AT THIS POINT, assuming that you have some capital and are ready to start investing in real estate to make money to achieve a better future, it would be a good idea to begin thinking about **how** you want to approach a real estate investment and **what** you want to get out of it. Putting some thoughts into this as the first step toward investing will indeed help you greatly in achieving the results you desire. As you begin to give this a serious thought, let me help you along by showing you how your approach to real estate investments depends on the kind of investor you really are.

1. **As a Passive Investor** – This person provides cash to a real estate investment company, allowing them to invest it on the person's behalf. For example, the money may be used to

indirectly hold rental or development property by purchasing shares in a real estate fund or by holding a silent partner position in a joint venture project. It involves a fund manager, a broker or a financial advisor who will act on your behalf to earn you interest, dividends or rental income. You are called a passive investor because you do not actively make decisions on where the money is invested.

2. **As an Active but Hands-Off Investor** – This person wants to make money by having ownership of property but does not want to be involved in the day-to-day management of the investment. This usually means investing in a rental property and hiring someone else as your property manager to manage the property for you by giving up a small percentage of the monthly rental income as payment for his or her service.

3. **As an Active but Hands-On Investor** – The only difference between a hands-off active investor and a hands-on active investor is the level of involvement. Being hands-on, you manage your own rental properties. You collect rent, maintain the property, find renters and do all the legwork yourself. And you get to keep all the money.

Some of you may ask, "How do I enter real estate if I have limited income?" It is a reality that many people live from paycheque to paycheque, so how do they find the capital to invest in real estate? This is where courage comes in. You have to approach family members or trusted friends to borrow the money needed. Or get a loan. If you are not able to get a loan, then apply for a home equity line of credit. Many of my clients are in similar situations when they come to me so I think outside the box and explore with them all kinds of financial options. For example, you can gain access to funds for capital by doing a joint business venture with a trustworthy family member or a very close friend. In cases when my clients are self-employed, since it is often very difficult for them to qualify for loans, I would help them by getting creative in finding partners for them.

"Where there is a will, there is a way" even if it seems that you do not have enough money to jump-start your journey into the real estate world.

Providing you have some capital already, a non real estate method to increase your money is by investing in stocks, funds, bonds and other traded securities. You basically earn money when dividends are issued over time or when you sell at a price higher than your buying price. This option requires you to have some understanding of the types of funds you intend to invest in, as well as some confidence in your selection decision As this generally requires a very long time horizon, you may be waiting a while before you see any gain. Also, if you attempt to shorten your horizon by speculating on the market, you risk the lost of your capital at the time you need it.

A riskier yet possibly lucrative non real estate method of increasing your money, is a method called "Hard Money or Private Lending". This is lending your money to people who desperately need it, and asking for a premium to be paid when the money is due to be returned. Banks use this same business model for making profit by letting consumers borrow money deposited by their customers for the purpose of buying big-ticket items like a car or a house or paying for services like a kitchen renovation or a construction project. The customer enters into a binding agreement to return the entire amount of the loan plus interest charged at a predetermined date. However, with "Hard Money or Private Lending", even if the loan is backed by hard assets, there is a risk of losing all of the money you lend out because the borrower may default, and the long-drawn-out legal process to get back the entire amount of the loan minus the fees associated with the process may still leave you with nothing.

Whether you are a passive or active investor, I cannot stress enough the immense importance of you knowing how money works in a tangible way. As I have already explained the difference between the **concept** of trading your time or possessions for money and the **concept** of making your money work for you without continuously giving up precious time or possessions, I hope you will boldly decide to make the necessary transition from your **usual way** of earning money by working to the **new way** I am pointing you towards. I know this whole transition process can be very daunting as it takes you out of your comfort zone where you solely earn a salary or a wage.

By now I hope I have successfully convinced you to embrace the latter concept, that is, the concept of making your money work for you without continuously giving up precious time or possessions. If so, let me help you start on this journey of creating your life's masterpiece by making your money work for you.

Movement IV:
Developing a Business Mindset

ANOTHER CRUCIAL THING to do before getting into the real estate world is to develop a business mindset. Only with this can your journey towards financial freedom begin.

What is a business mindset? To me, it is setting your mind to leverage resources and assets as well as to explore all options for growth and financial gain. It is important to develop this business mindset in order to enable yourself to search and especially to recognize opportunities around you. If you do not have this mindset, you can miss a great opportunity even if it is right under your nose.

Let me give you a real example by sharing the story of my clients **Eva and Henry** who are successful business owners in the software industry. They are both kind as well as ambitious people. Even though they were already financially comfortable before they came to see me, they felt lacking in the area of leaving a strong legacy for their children, so they were drawn towards investing in real estate. Because they have a business mindset, they were able to see that real estate was an opportunity for them to leverage their current finances and create more money in the hope of creating that legacy for their children.

So, how did they leverage their current finances? When they met me for a consultation, I provided them with clear directions on how to create a sizable real estate portfolio by leveraging all of their resources:

1. Pull equity out of their current principal residence by taking out a line of credit to use as a down payment on a vacant lot, and take out a mortgage on the lot to finance the construction of a larger residence there. Sell the old house upon moving into the new home, and use the proceeds to pay down the mortgage on the lot.

2. When the property value of the new home rises, pull equity out of it by obtaining a million-dollar line of credit.

3. Use the line of credit to re-invest by buying a strata office space for their business instead of continuing to rent one, and use the remaining funds to make further investments.

They followed my directions and successfully executed each and every step. After all that, they were able to not only create a legacy for their children but also build a house for their parents. That is the power of leveraging!

As you can see from this story, instead of continuously paying rent month after month for their business location, they switched to paying a mortgage every month and this creates sustainability as well as the room to grow. At the same time, Eva and Henry decided to partner with me on some multi-family condominium projects under Peak and Alture. It was such an ideal partnership as they were passive investors. This hands-off investment meant that they could earn a nice stream of income, while still running their own software business, and without having to worry about the welfare of their investments, as they were under the professional management of Peak and Alture from the start.

This is the outcome of leveraging whatever money you have at hand. Here, Eva and Henry are actually earning money with little risk by using the bank's money. With the initial money they have and the one house they own, they were able to sell and buy properties, and as a result, they started making more money. In short, their money multiplied!

I hope by sharing with you this couple's story, you will feel inspired to use leveraging as a means to making more money. I hope you will truly understand the power of leveraging money and start taking advantage of it to grow money in order to build wealth and attain financial security.

Eva and Henry entrusted me with their financial information and their heartfelt dream. They had total trust in my experience and ability to bring them closer to their financial goal. This trust is another type of business mindset, that is, utilizing other people's knowledge, skills and assets to make money. Eva and Henry leveraged my knowledge and skills, as well as the assets of both of my companies to grow their portfolio.

This is another aspect of the business mindset that you need to develop so that you can set your mind to explore all possible ways to grow financially. As soon as you have done that, you can thereby act on your motivation to reach the goal you have identified by looking around to see who can help you achieve that goal successfully. Eva and Henry now have new resources to help their business grow and more wealth to pass on to their children. They have created their life's masterpiece as I have, because now they can enjoy their life and live their dream by focusing all of their time and energy on their family instead of just their business.

Regardless of where you are financially right now, I hope you will develop a business mindset. You can certainly start by looking at the money and resources you have in a powerful way. That mindset will lead you to more opportunities than you can imagine. May your desire to fulfill your dream or pursue a passion motivate you to set a goal of achieving financial freedom and therefore, creating your own life's masterpiece.

Movement V:
Starting Your Investment Journey

WITH PROPER PROFESSIONAL structuring of your financing, and by enlisting expert professional consultation such as I have been and continue to provide to my clients, you would be on your way to owning real estate investments which have the ability to multiply your money, be prosperous and profitable, and to give you the cashflow that will carry you to a life of freedom from money-worries.

This is what I did for the following clients of mine who came to me for help because they wanted to invest in real estate with the limited savings they had:

- **Denise (Self-Employed and Renting)**

  Through my real estate business, I met Denise. She had attended a seminar that I held and approached me right after the event to express an interest in learning more about wealth. Not long after, we met again, and I am so glad to get to know her very well. She is now one of my friends. I am very happy to share her story.

Denise is an artist and an architectural designer. Art has always been her passion, but following this passion did not bring her the comforts she was looking for. She was, like any so-called starving artist, making an unstable income. This uncertainty tired her out and she so desired to be free of this just so that she could focus solely on all her artistic endeavours. But being self-employed, she felt trapped in a cycle of just making sure she had enough each month to pay bills. All her time was spent making sure she stayed afloat, and so consequently, she had no time or energy to dream big artistically. That frustration motivated her to look for a way out and it led her to one of my seminars. From my talk, she felt inspired, and I am so glad she approached me. Her hunger for a better life gave her strength to seek me out. She desperately wanted to break out of this cycle of just making ends meet. She just wanted freedom to pursue her art intensely, one hundred percent of the time.

Right off the bat, I encouraged her to take a chance in the real estate market, but she hesitated because she lacked confidence that this type of investment was within her reach. She only had a little bit of money saved up, and she was unable to get a bank loan due to her unstable income from self-employment. I helped her look over all possible options of getting the start-up funds for investment. And we found one — her boyfriend with a good credit rating. It warmed my heart to see that he was more than willing to help her out. Together, they qualified for a loan.

The plan I drew up for her based on her self-employment and financial situation was firstly to purchase a home in Surrey, British Columbia so that she did not have to pay rent anymore, and secondly, to rent out parts of her home to generate income to offset her expenses such as the interest incurred from her bank loan with her boyfriend.

The plan worked out successfully for her. In fact, it turned out so well that her confidence in real estate escalated. She felt empowered to go look for more properties to invest in and bravely asked me for further help to find more funds to enable her to own more income properties. And I found her a partner who was willing to pull funds together to join in this investment venture with her. Based on her first rental income and the new funds from that new partner, they were able to qualify for another loan which enabled her to buy more properties. I chose two properties in Dawson Creek, British Columbia for her because they were affordable, being located far away from the urban area. They were also high income-generating properties due to a strong rental market from the large workforce there extracting the area's natural resources. This research of mine uncovered this niche market which enabled her to enjoy a much higher cap rate than normal, in the double digits. A cap rate is the ratio of income over capital cost, and is expressed as a percentage, for example, 10%.

Because Denise had the courage to follow my plan, she was able to create a wealth portfolio comprising of one principal residence and two investment properties. Her confidence in real estate really grew quickly and now she feels secure over her finances. The best part of this story is the financial freedom she has achieved because she no longer lives just to make sure she has enough every month to pay her rent and bills. Ever since she started enlisting my help, the money she made enabled her to totally focus all her time and energy on her artwork. Why? Because both of her income properties are hands-off investments as they are being managed by Peak Performance Investments Ltd.

As of today, Denise's art business has brought her so much joy and satisfaction. Its success includes expansion of space and travels to various locations for projects that are interesting and exciting for her. She is now able to totally immerse herself in her passion for art and live her dream life because she has created her life's masterpiece from the financial freedom she has achieved. Her passion for art is no longer a reliance for earnings but a hobby. And she did it with just a little savings and with my help.

- **Ken (Student and Living with Parents)**

  I met Ken when he was nineteen. He was referred to me by another successful client of mine. For a few summers, he got a job on construction sites, doing framing work. He loved it so much that it became a passion and that was why he started dreaming of owning his own construction framing business. Being realistic, he knew he lacked knowledge on finances and therefore, could not see his own capability of ever reaching his dream. All he saw was his weaknesses and a wall of non-progress, both of which frustrated him. But his desire to do something about this frustration, plus his determination to not give up on his passion and dream motivated him to seek out advice from others in order to learn what to do about his current situation. That quest brought him to me.

Ken had heard about the potential of making money in real estate and so was very interested in entering this world. Right away in our first meeting, he asked a ton of questions about real estate investments. The following are some examples of his excellent questions:

- Which area is considered a good location for his first property investment?

- What type of property should he consider as a first-time investor?

- What are its potential returns?

At the time Ken came to me, he was still a student living at home, so he was able to save a lot of the money he earned from his summer framing jobs. In fact, he had about $20,000 stashed away which was incredibly impressive to me, coming from such a young adult. Many of such young people would have spent all or most of their money on partying and socializing, but instead he saved up. This self-control alone showed me his character. I knew right there and then that he would have the dedication needed to be successful in investing in the real estate world, and thereby would have no problem at all in creating more wealth to fulfill his dream of starting his own framing business.

It was no surprise to me that within an hour of consultation with me, he was ready to go ahead with the plan I had thought out for him. He was so ready to take risks and so very eager to get things rolling that within weeks, he made his first property purchase — a condo in Edmonton, Alberta. He obviously needed more than $20,000 for his down payment, so I got creative and found funds for him. Within just a few years, he had enough money to start his own construction framing company.

Today at age twenty-five, he owns not only a successful business with ten full-time employees but also six investment properties. And all that from just $20,000 to start with and at the young age of nineteen!

As you can see, whatever your age is and whatever amount of savings you have, as long as you have the desire to improve your current financial situation, you can. And if you do need guidance, assistance or support, you can find my contact information at the end of this book. My team will come up with a detailed plan specifically drawn for you to help you enter into the real estate world.

- **John and Amy (Townhouse Owners and Living with Stress)**

John and Amy have two young children and they used to live in a townhouse in Langley, British Columbia. They came to me frustrated and stressed out because they were struggling to provide for their children. The money from their jobs was barely covering all of their monthly expenses with little for their children's outside-the-school activities and certainly none for savings. This financial struggle caused the couple to fight daily over the issues of money which made me think about what their children were going through. Their experience reminded me so much about my own childhood days. I literally grew up watching and hearing my parents fight everyday nonstop about money. This fighting between my mom and dad over money really affected my outlook on life — that life is hard without money. It formed my approach to money and the managing of money which served me as I was growing up. I became determined to not only have enough to live on but also have extra so that I can live my life without stress. This determination drove me to seek ways to make sure that such stressful situations would never be repeated within my family and between my older folks these days.

Because I understood their predicament perfectly well, I was more than glad to be of help to John and Amy. During our consultation time, I guided them in identifying what their financial fears were and urged them to determine what they really wanted for themselves and their children. Basically, they feared losing money and they wanted financial freedom, just like all of us. So, I presented a few strategies to help expedite their wealth creation.

My very first recommendation was to sell the townhouse that they were living in at the time because I saw it as an expense. Their principal residence did not bring them any income because they were not able to rent out any part of their home. It only cost them money because of condo fees, maintenance fees and potential upcoming levies. They followed my recommendation and quickly sold off that townhouse and with the money from the sale, they listened to my suggestion of buying a fourplex (a building with four suites, each with its own entrance) so they could live in one unit and rent out the other three for rental income.

John and Amy followed through on my advice. Together with the money from the sale of their townhouse and the mortgage loan approved by the bank, they successfully bought themselves a fourplex with only a ten-percent down payment. Such arrangement allowed this couple to live in their unit essentially free of any cost, as their monthly rental income from the other three suites covered their monthly mortgage payment.

You can imagine the great positive impact of these strategies on their lifestyle. With no expenses like the ones they had incurred as owners of a townhouse, they began saving money. They no longer experience financial stress. Instead, they are enjoying financial security. They no longer fight. They are so happy to be able to meet their children's needs with ease.

Within just a span of two years, the value of that fourplex shot up by a whopping $150,000. I advised them to take advantage of this appreciation through equity financing based on the higher market value to buy another property. Without any hesitation, they took my advice and moved out of their own suite in their fourplex into a single detached house in Surrey, British Columbia. This property is a much larger home with not only more space and bedrooms for their growing family, but also containing a basement suite as well as a backyard carriage-home to generate extra rental income to cover the new mortgage payments. Now, they are enjoying being landlords and collecting rental income from a total of six rental sources.

Achieving financial freedom so that they can relax and spend more time with one another as a family instead of living with stress was my goal for this family and they reached it. This is exactly what I hope for you. I can help you like I have helped John and Amy with strategies specifically for you so you too can achieve a life of financial freedom.

- **Sonya (Employed and Surviving Paycheque-to-Paycheque)**

  I met Sonya not too long ago. She is extremely intelligent, very educated and quite successful in her career, but when she met me, she knew very little about wealth creation and suffered from what I saw as "a case of analysis paralysis" — overthinking every financial decision and refusing to take any risk! This refusal to act was costing her a lot of money because time is money. She and her husband were already struggling financially to begin with. So, the first thing I had to do to help her move towards wealth creation was to motivate her into action.

Sonya was a renter and had never thought about buying a house because of her reluctance to enter the real estate market. During our first consultation meeting, she was crying over the fact that she and her husband had not bought a house yet to provide a secure home for their daughter, and she felt very sure that they would never be able to buy one since they had no savings up to that point in time. I listened and focused on their strengths. While she and her husband were living from paycheque to paycheque, both of them had good jobs with good incomes which meant they could qualify for a line of credit.

It is true that the interest rate on the line of credit is a little higher than that on a loan, but it was a source of funds to enter into the real estate world. For them, I formulated a plan to leverage this line of credit to not only fund the down payments but also cover all the closing costs and legal expenses that came with the purchase of an amazing six different revenue-generating properties.

There were three components to this plan: (1) locating a niche market to capture a higher than normal cap rate; (2) taking advantage of the mortgage environment at the time of purchase to secure innovative and attractive financing; and (3) setting up a full property management package to gain the freedom of time. This plan worked out beautifully as it successfully churned out above average rental incomes from all these properties to cover all the interest payments on the line of credit. Before long, this consistent ability to pay monthly interest led to an increase in their credit rating and in turn, it increased the bank's confidence in their ability to pay interest which made it easy for me to help them switch to a mortgage with a lower interest rate, thus saving them money.

This is an effective strategy for people like Sonya who had no savings for a down payment because it is leveraging other people's money to creating wealth.

In a very short time after the purchase, each of their properties appreciated by at least twenty-five percent which meant Sonya and her husband automatically became wealthier. Since then, their investment portfolio has grown significantly and today, their net worth is well above a million dollars. They are creating their life's masterpiece as they are on the way to reaching financial security for the sake of their daughter. Their ultimate desire is to buy a principal residence to provide stability for the whole family and a more secure future. They are well on their way to fulfilling that dream.

Whatever your situation is, even if you have little to start, you can find your strengths to help you get out of your current financial status. Be it a crisis or a live-to-work-to-pay-bills trap or a case of analysis paralysis, there is a strategy which can be tailored just for you. The first move is the most crucial part. You have to want to do something about it. You have to decide to do something about it. Let me help you begin.

Movement VI:
Choosing to Earn Without Having to Be There

ONE OF THE main reasons why real estate is so attractive is that you can earn monthly income without spending much of your time or energy. You simply purchase a house and rent it out to generate monthly income. I have shared how my clients with different financial standing and situation have been able to enter this real estate world and how entering it provides an effective solution to solving their money problems. And now I want to show you how it leads to you having more money and more time.

Patty is another successful story about how one can choose to have income earned this way, resulting in more time at hand, enabling dreams to be pursued full-time. This is a case of **investing in real estate and being a hands-off landlord by entrusting the management to a professional firm.** Patty, through my companies, Peak Performance Investment and Alture Properties, did just that, and is now profiting from a regular income stream while enjoying time with her family and indulging in her passions.

Patty is a beautician who runs a small business — a spa — in her own duplex home. She has always been glad to be able to pursue her career, but her choice also brought her a whole set of financial insecurities and challenges. No different from all other small business owners, her self-employment with an unpredictable cash flow made obtaining a loan much needed to grow her business very difficult. The hardest for her was not being able to fulfill her daughter's desire to get an out of town education. Any chance of getting out of this financial woe seemed bleak to her at the time.

Through a referral by a long-time investor of mine, I met Patty. Even though she was already a real estate owner of a duplex, she admitted she did not know much about real estate. All she knew was that she so badly wanted to create wealth. It was very obvious to me then that her desire for wealth-creation was driven by her plan to expand her business and especially her desire to afford her daughter's wish.

During consultation time, we created a plan. First-off, we capitalized on my good connections with certain financial institutions to obtain the financing needed. The funds were used as down payments to make several property purchases. With a joint venture with Peak Performance Investment, she is making money as a hands-off investor. Such investment arrangement allows her more time and energy to focus on her passion of being the best beautician in town and the best mom she can be to her daughter.

Since our consultation meeting, her life has changed dramatically. Today her wealth has grown substantially. She has been putting more funds to keep growing her business and she feels proud to be able to send her daughter to school with no problem. Patty's life changed for the better and this can also happen to any one of you who are reading this book.

I have to say it is a sad reality that some people think they should not invest in real estate just because they do not know much about it. This is definitely a major misconception or what I call "a faulty illusion". You do not necessarily need to be an expert to go into real estate investment. Like Patty, find an expert to team up with and you will start benefiting from leveraging the expert's resources.

Peak Performance Investment and Alture Properties are founded with various business partners for the purpose of helping people make money, and therefore build wealth with much ease. **Our philosophy is putting people first.** *When you come for an initial consultation, we will listen to your unique story first. Then we will help you in identifying your needs and your wants in the hope of finding the most important thing in your life. After determining your realistic financial goal, we will come up with a plan filled with strategies. This is how we guide you in building your own wealth portfolio successfully.*

Movement VII:
Leveraging Your Assets and Profiting

AS YOU CAN see from the few Movements before, investing in real estate provides various opportunities of making money. Also, you might have noticed that I have used the word "leveraging" repeatedly. It just means taking advantage of something tangible (like your own money or assets or someone else's) and intangible (like someone's time, knowledge, experience and expertise) in order to gain and benefit. It is a powerful tool to use for making money in real estate regardless of the financial level you are starting at.

When you use your **own savings** or the equity of your home (principal residence), you are leveraging your own assets to make more money.

When you use **other people's money** by borrowing from them or from the bank, you are leveraging their money to build your own wealth.

When you **go to an expert** on real estate investment, you are leveraging his or her experience, knowledge and expertise to begin making your way to financial security and freedom.

When you use a **real estate management company** to manage your investment properties while you enjoy regular incoming cash, you are leveraging its time to gain more time and money for yourself to spend in your business or home or for self-enjoyment.

So, leverage and take advantage. Make money to create your life's masterpiece. Create your future.

When you make money through real estate investments, you are considered to have made a profit. And there are seven different ways of making such profit which I have categorized into profit centres, each with its own strategy. Understanding these profit centres can help you leverage your current assets in the best possible way, and therefore, maximize your investment options.

The Seven Profit Centres of Real Estate

1. **Rental Income** – Investing in real estate provides monthly income and cash flow.

2. **Equity on Day One** – As soon as you buy a property, you own the value of the property at whatever it is worth at the time of purchase.

This means if the price paid is below the market price, you gain instant equity.

3. **Appreciation** – Your property increases in value over time because of the depreciation of currency and the increasing demand of a growing population around the area, assuming that the purchase is in a location that supports new immigration and job growth.

4. **Leverage** – Real estate is in an asset class that is secure. That is why banks are willing to lend you money to invest in real estate. Utilizing the bank's money or any willing investor's money to increase your net worth is the mindset of a clever and strategic entrepreneur.

5. **Tax Benefit** – The fact that a real estate investment is considered a business, when you report your tax, you can deduct all direct expenses like property taxes, insurance, property management fees and repairs from any income generated from the investment.

6. **Mortgage Offset** – When you are a landlord, the natural thing to do is to use your tenant's monthly rental payment to you to decrease your mortgage principal (the outstanding balance of your mortgage) as well as to cover its monthly interest payment so that your entire

mortgage can be offset (paid off) over time and the property become yours with a free and clear title. Also, you begin to enjoy pure cash flow.

7. **Re-investment** – Instead of selling your property to make a profit, you may pull the equity out of it by refinancing it and using the available money to invest in more properties. This method of re-investing saves you money indirectly as you are using your tenants' rental money to pay down your mortgages. This is a process of growing your investment portfolio strategically.

I sincerely hope I have already successfully convinced you that anybody can make an investment in real estate and that it really is one of the easiest ways of earning recurring income which eventually leads to financial security. When you start making profits off your real estate investments, you can decide to keep or quit your nine-to-five job. All of my clients chose to spend all or most of their time focusing on their passions and fulfilling their dreams. Whatever your desire or motivation lies, whether it is to build assets for yourself to achieve a certain financial status or to create wealth for you to leave to your children or merely to earn extra income to spend or share, the decision and the choice are yours alone to make.

Movement VIII:
Applying My Nine Principles of Success

I TRUST THAT by now you have learnt how to invest in real estate and make money in order to be financially free. Although it is confidence that I want to build in you, I do need to caution you at this point about the reality of achieving financial security — that it can take a long time before you see it and it is not as easy as it sounds. Achieving financial security absolutely requires patience, time and understanding.

As you know now that it took my company Alture two years to begin experiencing some momentum. The most important point is what we did during those two years of waiting. While we were receiving continuous stream of cash flow using Strategy #1 (Buy and Hold), we kept working diligently by executing other strategies to improve our investors' returns. We made sure we did not waste time waiting for success to happen based on one investment or one strategy. We kept getting creative for the company and for our clients. We understood the value of time by working continuously while patiently waiting to see what our decisions would bring us. You can do the same while you wait to see the fruition of your investment. This time aspect is an important part of being a successful real estate investor.

Because of this time aspect, I have formulated what I call my "Nine Principles of Success" for you to utilize on a practical basis. You will benefit from them as they are based on all that I have experienced and learnt during my own quest of success. They can be applied at any time or at any point of your life.

Nine Principles of Success

1. Visualize What You Want

Are you familiar with the concept of visualization? Olympic athletes use it to see themselves in their own head winning gold. They do this as they are getting themselves ready to compete. Gymnasts, with eyes either open or closed, would go through their entire routine, moving their arms and legs in their imagination. But really, it is not just the movements they are visualizing. It is also the feel of the air against their skin when tumbling up and down and flipping around and around, the hearing of the crowd cheering for them, the smelling of the chalk on their hands and the touching down of their feet on the gymnastics mats on the floor. This mental exercise engages all of their senses to visualize what they truly want to see happen in real life.

I once had a discussion with a personal trainer who used to train gymnasts. I wanted to know how she has been coaching them in visualization. Is it in the first person or in third person? Do they visualize as if they themselves were performing the movements or as if they were watching themselves perform the movements? Her answer was both. She said visualizing in both the first person (staying within yourself and feeling yourself actually performing) and the third person (stepping outside of yourself to see yourself performing) are equally necessary in effectively preparing for an actual performance.

I would like you to take a brief moment to apply the same technique in your real estate investments. Whether you are working in an office in a tall tower or sitting on the beach using your laptop to write a great American novel or making million-dollar deals or designing buildings, just pause for a minute...close your eyes and visualize yourself earning a regular stream of money from your hands-off investments, and enjoying that money and time by doing things you love. Visualize something that you long to have or something you long to experience because you have achieved the financial means for it. Visualize in the first person or visualize in the third person — it does not matter as long as you close your eyes and take full note of your feeling, hearing, smelling and seeing all that is around you.

Visualization is a powerful tool to use to help us stay in the waiting game of real estate invest-ments. Why? Because it trains our brain to expect success and taste profit to keep us in this game. It is a good thing that our brain actually cannot tell whether what we see in our imagination is real or made-up, but it can cer-tainly still make a connection somehow from our imagination to our belief so that it affects our decision-making. I used this technique when my goal of having my own songs on the Billboard was a mere dream. Daily without fail, I visualized myself playing the piano and writing a Billboard-worthy song and winning awards. These imaginations were so very real to me that they became real because this exercise helped me make a real concerted effort in using my time to reach my Billboard goal. This is an important principle to adopt if you want to stay on course towards success.

Let me share how I have been putting visualization into practice to feel more connected to my dreams. Have you heard of a vision board? I have been calling mine a **dream board** instead because it is fully covered with **pictures of everything that I ever wanted in life** — material things like a house or a car and experiences like getting an award for songwriting. Go ahead and create your own dream board too using pictures of tangible things that you want or pictures that are symbolic of lifestyle. For example, if you want to live a more balanced life, you can use a picture of a scale to represent balance or a picture of a flower to represent both serenity and balance. Search through magazines for cut-outs or online for printouts. When you pin up these cut-outs or printouts onto your dream board, write words right under each picture to remind yourself what your dreams are. And you can also cut out strips of words from printed materials to paste anywhere on the board to inspire you to make every effort to move towards achieving those dreams and goals.

People tend to hang their dream board out in the open to be seen every day, but not me. I found it much more effective to have my dream board tucked away out of sight only to be pulled out once a year to be looked at. It is more fun this way as I get to see what I have actually accomplished in a year and I get to count how many dreams have come true. Anyhow, it is entirely up to you to decide whether to have yours tucked away or displayed in the open. Do whatever works for you.

As you begin your real estate investments, it is not too early to start visualizing as far as what you want to do when you obtain success. It is really important that you make this exercise of visualization a part of your daily routine. It is also very fitting to incorporate it with journaling. Whichever way you choose to visualize, this principle truly can help you stay positive while you wait for the fruition of your investments. It sets your whole self up to attain what you desire for your life, making sure that you stay on track with what you have in mind in the first place.

2. Believe That You Can Have It

When you have a dream, believe that you can have it. Take time to identify everything that is holding you back from chasing this dream. At the same time, find time to figure out why you want to pursue this dream. **This discovering process can help you succeed in reaching your dream as it reaffirms your actions and decisions** on investments, thereby making you feel very confident and capable in multiplying money to get you closer to living your dream. If these mental exercises still could not help you see beyond failures and difficulties, then it is crucial that you find someone who can cheer you on and keep giving you the support you need to succeed.

Surrounding yourself with as many positive and supportive people as possible who believe in you is truly very important in achieving success. For me, as I was growing up I wanted to succeed in piano and songwriting, My piano teacher told my mom that I was a prodigy. She believed in me and I believed her. From the beginning, my mother and my piano teacher have been cheering me on continuously as I achieved success. Now that I am an adult running my own business as a consultant, I have my most wonderful husband and my pretty cool son supporting and encouraging me to pursue my other dreams.

3. Be Inspired to Take Rapid Actions

Let me share with you a story about a seminar that I attended when I was twenty-one years old. Tony Robbins was the featured speaker. Since my younger days, I have been listening to him and am still an avid fan of his. I believe in the things he has been teaching and I try to follow him faithfully. At the time of the seminar, I was still in university and only working part time, so $800 a ticket to the seminar was a lot of money. However, in spite of this situation, I went ahead and bought a ticket anyway because I felt inspired to do so. I took action by following my gut instinct.

Up to that point in time, I had never been to a seminar and so I did not know what to expect at all. When I arrived there, all I could see was a very huge crowd and an extremely long line-up. I remember saying anxiously to myself, "Holy smokes! By the time I get my turn in the line, I will be in the nosebleed section. That is too far from the speaker." At the spur of the moment, I decided to bypass the entire line and confidently walked right in. I went straight to the VIP section and sat down in the front row. I was very pleasantly surprised that nobody stopped me. In fact, a staff-member came by only to tell me that the front row was reserved for Tony's family, and so I just thanked her and moved to the second row and sat down right in the middle. I remained there the whole entire time. And what an inspiring, life-changing seminar.

How is that for being inspired to take a rapid action at the right moment? The $800 was well worth it and the decision to bypass the line-up was rewarding. If you have not heard about Tony Robbins before reading this story of mine, I want to encourage all of you to check him out by reading his books or going to his seminars. You only stand to gain from his enormous knowledge.

Being inspired to take rapid actions means **listening to your gut instinct and act immediately without doubting yourself or second-guessing yourself.** The first time I made a real estate purchase, I acted on my gut instinct. I had no idea what to expect or how things would turn out. I just jumped right in.

Applying this principle certainly requires a bit of faith and that can be difficult for some. Let me suggest how you can start living out this principle. Think of doing something, no matter how big or small, and right away, go get it done. For instance, you have been inspired to join a gym but still have not done so. Drop everything now and go join one. Procrastinate no longer! Another instance, you want to say hello to a certain someone for a long time now but have not plucked up the courage to do so. Wait no more! Go now to say hello. It is simply about moving to take action and not staying at the same spot forever. Some of you may have had the desire to start your own business since a while ago. What is stopping you? Be inspired and take rapid action.

4. Surrender to the Process

The main reason why I believe our dream board should be tucked away is because hanging it out on the wall for everyone to see is too much pressure. By having it out of sight, I can relax and surrender to the process of reaching a dream. This principle allows me to trust that I will eventually gain the things and experiences that are represented by the pictures posted onto my dream board at the timing that is right for me.

I had to wait two decades to achieve my dream of becoming a Billboard Songwriter. I believe everything worked out in the time frame meant for me. No matter who we are or what we do, we have to accept and embrace the timing of an outcome. The less stressed out you feel over the process of achieving success, the more likely you will want to hang on till the end to be rewarded. You just need to be relaxed, confident and patient because **in due time, success will come.**

Worry not about how you will arrive. Just take your first step. I tell you as I have told all of my clients, "The bridge that we need to walk across will be built for us only if we are brave enough to take the first step". I embrace this belief all my life and have integrated it throughout this book. As soon as you have taken that first step forward, surrender to the process and you will see results when you get there.

5. **Stay Focused**

Keep remembering what you want to achieve. I strongly recommend **using a journal or a planner** or both to write down what you want and to plan how you want to achieve it. Be flexible in your plan as sometimes new opportunities and possibilities can turn up that may require you to alter your course of action. At the odd times, someone may even enter your pathway to help you achieve success as well. Regardless, stay focused on what you want in the first place. Keep an eye on the prize.

6. Be Aware of Yourself and Listen to Your Instinct

Practise being aware of yourself. A good way I can suggest for you to start is by setting your watch to chime every hour. At every chime, take twenty or thirty seconds to check in on yourself by asking the following questions:

"How are you doing?"

"How are you feeling?"

"What are you thinking about?"

"Are your thoughts positive and productive or negative and destructive?"

"Are you taking steps today toward your ideal life?"

"If not, what is getting in your way?"

"How can you maneuver over, under and around this obstacle?"

This is how you will gain self-awareness. In time, you will be able to **recognize your own instinct and listen** to it. In real estate investments, this is an important principle to adopt in order to stay the course of achieving your goals.

7. Learn It, Try It and Practise It

Most people came to me for assistance in real estate investments because they had no clue in the first place. I am very glad to say that all of them sincerely wanted to learn and so they attended my seminars to get such an education. But knowledge is only knowledge until the person with the knowledge puts it to use willingly.

You can say you know how to knit, but if you never actually knit, then saying that you know is not very useful. Likewise, you can say you learnt how to swim from reading a book, but if you have never ever tried swimming in the water, how can you be sure you really know? You have to be willing to try what you have learnt, and practise and practise to perfect it.

The same is true when dealing with your passions or dreams. As a child, I was told by my piano teacher that I was a prodigy, born with a natural talent for playing the piano and writing music. But simply believing her words and just relying on my natural talent would not have been enough. For one, it would have made me lazy and take things for granted. Not practising my piano or not committing my whole being to hone my piano skills would have prevented me from accomplishing any of my goals later.

In other words, regardless of your natural talents, you still have to be willing to learn to gain more knowledge and be diligent in putting that knowledge into practice if you want to live out your passions or fulfill your dreams. Testing that knowledge is crucial in making sure that what you learn works for you, and that you are made to do that your whole life. Overall, when you apply this principle to your life, you will be able to affirm your true passions or dreams, and also ascertain that they have not changed over time because of age or new experiences.

This process of learning, trying and practising is **the process of improving and it should bring you enjoyment.** If you are not enjoying it, then you are surely on the wrong path, because when you are on the right path, you just feel energized, motivated and satisfied.

So, go learn, try and practise to find the right path. It will help you to stay on the path to achieving great success in your life, and in this case, in your real estate investments.

8. Choose Who You Surround Yourself With

I mentioned the importance of having a support system in the second principle. Let me expand on that here by sharing with you my own personal story in getting to where I am today.

Right out of college, I opened my own music business and was faced with having to make some very tough decisions in order to push myself to stay on course. I knew I had to take risks if I wanted to achieve my goals of success. With growth as one of my goals at the time, I decided to rent a business location, hire a receptionist and set up an overall operational system instead of saving money to run it from my home.

Today, I am very proud to say that Mozart School of Music is thriving with many music teachers employed and many students getting top-notch professional music instruction. And it is no longer paying rent as I now own the building that it is located in today.

But this did not happen overnight and it almost did not happen at all. I always have tons of ideas, but at that time, being unsure of myself, I just could not see how I was going to use any of them. Like any other business entrepreneur, starting this music business was a huge risk, especially since I was just a fresh college graduate. I hesitated a lot then, even though deep down I knew somehow it would work out.

How I overcame my hesitation and lack of confidence was the support of a good friend,

Jennifer. She really believed in me and encouraged me. She even went an extra mile to support me by partnering with me to get this music business started. I am so grateful that I had her around me during that period of my life.

All of us will meet at least one person who will become key to us in deciding which path we end up walking on. But we have to do our part. We must be humble to **accept his or her help.**

If you are working, look for help from mentors in your industry. If you have a business, gather people who believe in you and build a supportive team who can be there to help you be unstoppable. If you think you cannot find anyone supportive to surround yourself with, I suggest you try looking for one by taking the initiative to get to know your friends and acquaintances well.

Another way of feeling like you have support is by attending seminars organized by authors and meeting them in person to learn from them. In any case, if and when you have friends who are good to you, be sure to keep them close to you and be good to them as well and never take them for granted. Be grateful always and be sure to show your unequivocal appreciation for their support and belief in you.

On the flip-side, make sure you let go of those who are pure "energy-drainers" for they can pull you down and distract you from your goals.

Choosing to surround yourself with the right people is an important principle to adopt. This can be a make-it-or-break-it point in obtaining financial freedom which is ultimately your goal as you get into real estate investments.

9. Go Forth with Confidence

When you have taken that first step to make your first investment in real estate, pat yourself on the back for taking courage to move forward. It is the same courage needed to pick up a form for you to fill in and register your business or a paintbrush to start painting. I urge you to start now, if you are still in the considering stage. For those of you who have already begun, my congratulations to you.

The principle here is to go forth with confidence. When that first step is being taken, **inhale confidence and exhale doubts and fears and face forward.** Whatever has inspired you to take that step, let it keep you going until you reach your goal.

I highly recommend that you read through these nine principles of success repeatedly so that you can commit them to memory. Print them out and place them in a location where you have to walk by everyday so that you can often remind yourself of their value. Integrate them into your dream board.

When you have fully applied every single one of these principles of success into your daily life, you will see yourself letting go and relaxing more while waiting to taste success.

In due time before you know it, that prize of your success will arrive at your doorstep at the right time and at the right place of your life. If you need further help in understanding and applying these nine principles, you may contact my team anytime.

Movement IX:
Enjoying Financial Freedom

WHAT DOES IT mean to you to be financially free? What does financial freedom look like to you? What do you want to do when you achieve it? While you take a few minutes to seriously think about your answers to these questions, let me share with you three different people's view of financial freedom and how achieving it changed their lives.

- **Dr. Szeto (Dentist with a Change of Heart)**

  My client Dr. Szeto is a dentist by profession. When he came to see me, he had a well-established practice in Langley, British Columbia, and was doing quite well financially. Even though he was living his dream and earning good money, deep down he was not satisfied. Somehow his profession did not seem meaningful anymore. He felt that he was not making any impact on the world by just looking after his patients' teeth. He felt that he could do so much more to make a lasting difference in a person's life. He apparently has changed. Being a dentist is no longer his passion. Over time, he developed a new one — public speaking. But he was not free to pursue it because he needed to keep his practice going.

That was the reason why he sought my help. His profession was bringing in money, but it was not building wealth for him and his family. He had heard about real estate and its power to create wealth. So, he started thinking this path might be the right one for him to take since he wanted to create more wealth for his family.

We met and discussed all kinds of possible investments for him. Before long, Dr. Szeto bought two townhouses in Fort St. John, British Columbia and subsequently a fourplex in Surrey, British Columbia. These investments provided him with a consistent cash flow every month. The market value of the fourplex has increased because the property is situated in an area where development of condos is under discussion. Furthermore, he has been receiving multiple offers from developers for his fourplex, which gives him the upper hand in choosing which offer to accept. In other words, he has struck gold.

Dr. Szeto's life has been very different ever since he entered real estate. He has found financial freedom. Such freedom has allowed him to stop depending on his practice to bring in income for him to provide for his family. It has instead given him the option to pursue his new love for public speaking which gives him the satisfaction of seeing his motivational words making an impact on people's lives. He used to join a monthly seminar group to learn all he could about real estate investments. Nowadays, he is instead hosting a group and teaching others about real estate investments. This has brought him fulfilment into his life by being able to share his knowledge on wealth-building strategies and tell his own success stories. This financial freedom is providing him the luxury of time to pursue his newfound passion because he is utilizing the expertise of a professional property management company as partners in a joint venture.

- **Francesca (Public School Teacher about to Retire)**

  Francesca became my client a few years before she retired as a public teacher because she was very worried about not having enough to live on later. She had already chosen a frugal lifestyle, and because she was nearing retirement, she consciously had been cutting back on spending just to save up. She wanted to make sure she could continue to have enough funds to afford her the means to explore life after retirement. She had many interests which she wanted to pursue, and she was very concerned about possible unexpected medical expenses down the road.

Following my advice, she initially made some short-term investments because she wanted the flexibility to utilize these funds during the first 5 years of her retirement. For her longer term horizon, we began searching for investment opportunities that would give her maximum cash flow with minimal risk because she had expressed how important cash flow would be to her as a retiree due to her long to-do list.

We were able to find two properties in Dawson Creek for her to purchase. These were half-duplexes that brought multiple income streams from the upper and lower tenants. When she came to me, she had already owned a home sitting on a large developable lot. I saw an opportunity for her to make a profit, and advised her to sell part of her lot without having to move from her home. She agreed, so we were able to help carve up one side of the land, and sell it to an interested developer. So, in addition to the new rental incomes, she had this huge lump sum of money to enjoy.

Doing these investments has helped her retire comfortably without any worry or stress. The transition from being employed to being retired was smooth because she felt financially secure. The money from the partial land sale and from her rental properties is allowing her to do exactly what she has always wanted to do. She got to renovate her kitchen, participate in lots of outdoor sports and even pick up motorcycle riding as a hobby. It so happened later that she did have to face some medical challenges and had to undergo operations. While she lay resting at the hospital for a long period of time, she felt at ease, knowing that her finances remained intact.

Financial security to Francesca meant having genuine peace of mind and confidence as she entered another stage of her life. Now as a retiree, her wealth afforded her the opportunity to upgrade her lifestyle and it also provide a safety net to tackle any future medical concerns.

Francesca's story showcases what financial independence looks like for those of you who are nearing retirement. We all want to look forward to an early retirement life, doing the things we dream about, when we have all the time in the world. There is success in real estate investments regardless of age. Start NOW...it is never too late.

I personally know of many grandparents and parents who have worked hard at jobs they disliked, just to save money. Their hearts desired to move to an area they always dreamt to live in or to travel around the world to enjoy life. But sadly, they could never seem to save up enough, and so they kept working until their passing.

For those of you who are such hardworking people in a job or a career you either like or dislike and with such desires at heart, I truly want a different path for you. I hope this book can convince you to make the choice to invest in real estate to create the wealth you deserve.

- **Me, Myself and I (Entrepreneur Full of Ideas)**

  For me, achieving financial freedom means having the money and time to freely pursue my childhood dreams so that I could create my own life's masterpiece. I followed every single one of my 9 principles of success, and so I am extremely proud of myself for successfully achieving the financial freedom I aimed for right from the start.

This freedom allowed me the opportunity to pursue my love for songwriting. I traveled to Hong Kong and was able to dedicate five years of my life to pursue my songwriting career. It had been very satisfying because three of my compositions made it to the Top-Ten most played songs on Billboard and two of them won trophies for Best Original Song. I also was nominated for "Song of the Year" by the largest music organization in Hong Kong. It was such a dream come true as I travelled throughout Asia as a celebrity with the privilege of staying at 5-Star hotels and the opportunity to meet many famous musicians and producers.

This freedom has also allowed me to change my mind about pursuing my songwriting career full-time and come back to Canada. I am grateful for the income from my real estate investments which has given me the ability to take up the following endeavours:

- Holding regular **seminars** to share my knowledge, experience and ideas in hope of inspiring people to achieve not only their financial goals but also their life's goals.

- Putting together a **yearly concert** to share my songs and story, such as my Broadway style production "Seasons, a Magical Musical".

- Getting this book written and published for you. 100% of my royalties from the sale of this book goes to the **Wendy Yau Sum Cheung Fund** at the Capilano University to provide scholarships each year in perpetuity to qualifying music students.

Do you identify yourself with any of my real life examples in terms of defining financial freedom? Today, such freedom to my clients simply means having options. They are free to choose what they want to pursue so they can still spend time with the people they love. It means having choices on how to utilize their money and time. Is that what financial freedom means to you? Your answer will show you your desires and also reveal your truest passions and your deepest dreams.

I advise you to be open to all possibilities. When you achieve financial freedom, you will have not only money but also time. The following are some ideas on how you can enjoy them:

- Taking a world cruise while enjoying butler service from your private suite.

- Organizing charitable events for a cause closest to your heart.

- Walking the cobblestone streets of Paris, taking in the fragrance of freshly baked baguettes while admiring the monumental stature of the Eiffel Tower.

- Enjoying the classic works of the Masters played by the Philharmonic Orchestra in the opulent Great Hall in Vienna.

- Being a full-time volunteer as a contributing citizen.

- Taking care of a close family member by hiring help.

- Starting a community farm out of a strong belief for local sustainability.

- Opening up a school in a third world country to teach children who otherwise will not have the opportunity to have a proper education.

I have met a few people who are a bit overwhelmed by all the possibilities this vast financial freedom offers. When you have been living a life filled with routines and never-ending demands, an easier and better lifestyle sounds very unrealistic and too good to be true.

I encourage you to start planning. What will you do when you get the time to do what you love? Today, what will you start working on to help yourself move towards living that ideal lifestyle? Let me try and help you get started. Spend 15-20 minutes a day sitting still with your eyes closed for these exercises of imagination: (a) Dream about the life you want; and (b) Visualize how you will feel when you have money and time. Then open your eyes and quickly write down everything your mind has revealed without judgement. Let yourself honor your own wishes, your desires and your ambitions. Most of all, hear your own yearning. Listen to your passionate voice that speaks to you when you let go of your own fear or worries.

Write your wishes down as if you only had 10 days left to live on this planet. After you finish writing all that you can without any pausing, take some time to review what you have written. Appreciate yourself for taking the time to plan out what a better and more fulfilling life looks like to you personally. Give yourself the acknowledgement you need. Try to figure the first step you can take to help yourself realize your plan of actions and take it! For example, if you want to start a business, register a domain name or if you want to learn a new subject, register for a course or if you want to learn how to create wealth in real estate, start following the steps in this book. Visualize everyday to remind yourself why you want what you want in the first place.

The key thing is not to be stuck in the thinking and planning stage. To make sure your thoughts and plan materialize, you must take timely actions. Right away, take the initiative to start toward achieving your financial security. Truly embrace and master my nine principles of success. Undoubtedly, you will begin to see consistent and positive progress toward living the life you visualized.

Movement X:
Creating and Sharing Your Own Concerto

WHEN I LOOK around at people who are happy and successful in life, I cannot help myself but get drawn to them, especially those who are not only grateful for what they have, but also for what they can actually give back to the world. I believe in the amazing power of gratitude and that its effects are immeasurable. I myself have experienced its power when my friend generously helped me commercialize my first business. I can see that she appreciated what she had. Out of that appreciation, she wanted to help me. She expressed her belief in me by investing the funds which I needed to turn my home-based business of providing one-on-one music lessons into a commercial-based business with a retail front and signage. I am grateful for her help to take my business to this next level with the ability to create employment for many music teachers to provide music lessons to many students at the same time. Since then, I expanded my business further by successfully leveraging my brand, The Mozart School of Music, through creating franchise opportunities.

Now it is my turn to show gratitude by helping others. It's like creating my own concerto to share my music with my audience. Her generosity has left a lasting effect on me. It has driven my motivation and desire to help others achieve financial freedom so that they too can create their own life's masterpiece. Also, in giving, you are always blessed ten times more because you feel happy, and this makes your day as you see how your generosity makes a difference in people's lives. I know when I receive that standing ovation after performing my concerto, my audience appreciates my sharing of my music with them, and that I have made a difference in their lives.

There is so much for us to give and to share all around. If you are still saying, "There's not enough money" or "There's not enough time", then you have not counted your new income streams from rentals or the lump sum of money from the sale of a property as blessings. Be thankful for the wealth you have just created and start showing your appreciation by giving back. Find a cause that is close to your heart. Or support a charity that aligns with your values.

Give back because it is good for you.

Why is it good for you? When you give back:

- you feel better about yourself, your accomplishments and your wealth.

- you learn about yourself and about others. What a golden opportunity!

- you make valuable connections with people who may have the power to change your outlook on life and reveal to you some amazing things.

- It changes your focus in life as you move the focus from you to another person.

When your heart is full of gratitude, compassion and generosity, you will see yourself enjoying what you have much more. At the same time, your persona becomes richer, smarter and more attractive to those around you. You truly have the power to change the world and make it better by giving back. And you give back by sharing who you are, what you have and what you know.

This Movement, even though it is not talking about making money or real estate investments, it is just as important as all the other Movements. I hope after you have finished reading it, you will understand its immense importance. Can you try and think of people who you know who are happy and successful? What do you notice about them? I have found most of them to be people who are grateful for what they have. Their gratefulness is shown in their kindness to others, their willingness to volunteer their time and in their readiness to donate their money. If we are grateful, we will be generous and giving.

So, what are you grateful for? Start with your family and their unconditional love. Then remember your friends who are always there for you. Make thankfulness part of your life by sharing what you have with others because you are now at a place where money is no longer an issue.

Once you have achieved financial freedom, it is extremely important to have the right people by your side and surrounding you. Do not keep to yourself nor be alone when you have attained wealth. Let someone keep you accountable. It can be an investment realtor, a mortgage specialist, a lawyer, an insurance broker, a property manager and even a business and wealth coach whom you can see from time to time to keep you in check. This is part of gratefulness is important because it shows that you realize, without a good team, it is difficult to make it to the top financially. For those of you readers who will become successful and wealthy one day, make sure you give back to the people and the community who have made a difference in your life.

If you want to create your life's masterpiece and have a better future, you need to design the way you want it to look like. To speed the process up, get in touch with my team of professionals who are dedicated to making a difference in your life by supporting you in reaching your financial goals, attaining entrepreneurial growth, striving for personal development and even attempting any artistic endeavors. On the last page of this book, I have listed the contact information of all of my current companies for you. Feel free to get in touch with me anytime.

I hope this book has given you what you were intended to find and that it has inspired you to think about your future and desire to create it by creating your life's masterpiece. Thank you for buying this book and reading it. Pay it forward by sharing it with someone whom you think can benefit as well. I look forward to meeting you one day soon.

Finale:
My Music Box of Treasures: Thirty-Six Gems to Encourage and Inspire You

em 1   *Compress Time.* Time is limited, no matter how rich we are. Just as we always take the shortest route to get to a place we want to go, we should always find the most efficient method to get something done. How? By leveraging off existing platforms and by going to where the action is and learning from the masters.

em 2   *Believe It Is Easy.* Doing things can be easy if you believe that to be. Since our brain is able to be tricked, if we genuinely believe within our mind that something is easy, then it no longer appears difficult. There-

fore a challenging process becomes much easier to accomplish.

 Think Outside the Box. Take on new ideas that others have not tried. It is alright to invent the wheel. The more creative and innovative we are, the more solutions we can bring to the table.

 Get Over being Judged — the Only Way to Grow. We all want to be loved because love is an essential human need. But there are people in our lives who cannot show their love to us even if they do love us. Or perhaps when they express it, we do not see it. Sometimes, we get judged on something which we don't believe within our mind that we should be judged on. We grow by getting over these judgements..

 Choose Fear or Action. Fear is a real emotion. Letting it paralyze you is a choice you make unconsciously. The best way to conquer fear is to learn to face it. The best way to overcome it is by taking action.

 Calculate the cost of Not Doing versus Doing. There is a cost for lying around and doing nothing. Likewise, there is a cost for seizing opportunities. Both correlate to our energy input. If we want something to change, we must first change ourselves. If we want to preserve what we have, we need to review what we have and keep maintaining status quo. It is important to know that constant efforts are required in order to strive for success and keep it. It is the price you pay and you are the only person who knows if it is worth it or not. The reward can be more than what you expect.

 em 7 ***Grow by Surrounding Yourself with More Successful People.*** Always be with people who will motivate you to be the better version of your current self. The question is whether they are willing to be with you. If they are, take advantage of that opportunity! Learn from them and grow.

 em 8 ***Make YOLO = Make Your Only Life Outstanding!*** Since you have only one life to live, you owe it to yourself to make it the best! Why shortchange yourself?

 em 9 ***Find Reasons to Succeed.*** We often talk ourselves out of walking forward due to

fear and doubts that we made up so that we can make ourselves feel better about quitting. This is a fallacy. Re-frame your mind and listen to stories about winning, and keep everything congruent all the way until you reach your destiny.

 10   *Operate by Sight.* When we are positive, we see things as advantages and we recognize people who can help us. On the other hand, when we are negative, we see everything as an obstacle. Our feelings dictate our day-to-day outcomes. Therefore, generate only positive feelings as much as you can daily through self-affirmations, inspiring music and uplifting books.

 11   *Be CRAZY — "No Logic" Phenomenon.* Sometimes being a little crazy is a good thing. We do not need to always analyze everything in order to make a decision. We have internal instincts which can also guide us if we follow spontaneously. Be intuitive and listen to your inner voice. Go with the flow.

12   *Set OUTRAGEOUS Lofty GOALS.* Making five million dollars in Canada from

my businesses and hitting the billboard in Hong Kong with the songs I wrote were my goals at age 18. There was no logic to it and no strategies at that point in time. But our mind is more powerful than we can actually imagine. Always set goals and write down detailed objectives that will motivate us to take actions. Mark our milestones to inspire ourselves to keep going.

 Gem 13 ***Do Not Get Stuck in the Moment.*** Sometimes we hit rock bottom and feel uninspired. I have to tell you that these moments are just temporary. Keep imagining that you are seeing the sun shining and keep going non-stop. Do not let these momentary setbacks define who you are. Keep making an effort to keep on track. Do not throw away any progress. If necessary once in a while, give yourself permission to take a break.

Gem 14 ***See a Bridge Appear When You Have the Courage to Walk.*** There is always a way out when you come to an end. A classic Chinese proverb says: "When the boat gets to the head of a bridge, it will naturally straighten itself out".

em 15 ***Be Focused, Passionate, Dedicated and Diligent.*** We need to concentrate in order to get results. To continue to stay focused, we need to pick up something we are passionate about. For example, in my business, I am dedicated to continuing to improve what I have so that I can refine our processes and implement new ways to build efficiency. In terms of quality, being diligent is one of the most important elements needed to obtain the highest degree of standards.

 em 16 ***Do Trial and Error.*** We learn from our experiences that come from both good and bad decisions. They become our building block for future successes. So, do not shy away from making decisions because of your fear of an undesirable outcome. It is far better to take a risk on making a bad decision than to make no decisions at all and sit on the fence.

em 17 ***Believe You Can Have It All.*** Do not short-change yourself by believing that you have to choose between two options. You can have both. Whenever you have to decide, try to find a way that gives you the best of both worlds. For instance, you can choose

to take care of your family full-time while keeping a hobby alive or choose to go back to college while running a business. Always aim to give yourself that third option of choosing both.

em 18 ***Have a Good Relationship with Money.*** Your mind will attract the things you want and repel the things you do not want. I trust money is something you want, so be open to receiving more of it.

em 19 ***Believe that One Day All is Going to Come Together.*** Sometimes you may not know why you are doing what you are doing. You also may not know why certain people show up at certain times of your life and why they leave at some point in time. But I believe one day you will see that everything will be part of a master plan where the dots themselves show up to reveal the whole picture on your canvas.

em 20 ***Understand Success.*** I trust that you have read and learnt the Nine Principles of Success found in Movement VIII of this book. Live by them. Progress from learning to implementing daily if you want success.

21   *Embrace the Unknown.* The unknown can be intimidating and at the same time, powerful. Your confidence will strengthen you to take action for something that has not materialized yet. Many artists hone their skills before they get the opportunity to showcase their talent. When that opportunity arrives, that is the moment they get to shine and make headway. Like a professional chef, keep sharpening your knife, for you never know when you need it. When the time comes, you would not want to waste it on wishing you could have been prepared and ready for the moment.

 22   *Choose the Path of Least Resistance.* Sometimes we try too hard to get something. Take the easy and no-struggle approach. Let things naturally happen before your eyes and just say yes to it. Oftentimes we sabotage our opportunity due to our own insecurities, complexity and self-doubt. Stop it altogether! Just enjoy walking on the path, and be grateful that you can walk, and be thankful for that path to walk on.

23   *Pay for Expertise.* Pay an expert for his or her time and advice. Trial and error costs

a lot. Receiving mentorship is invaluable, especially from those people who are experienced in the field in which you want to enter! You have to understand that it will take years and years for you to know what they already know. Therefore, it is best for you to have smart people on your team before you roll out your ideas.

 em 24 ***Build Lasting Relationships within Business.*** Employing people is part of growing your business. Most crucial is finding the right people for the right tasks. You get no productivity by putting someone in a place where he or she does not belong. Make sure you give the right position to the right candidate and the match will last a long time, even for life. Lasting relationships within your business help it achieve much success.

em 25 ***Celebrate Each and Every Milestone!*** Take it a step at a time and reward yourself along the way. The progress you see will continue to drive you towards success. Write it in a diary to keep track of all the little successes. Make sure you pat yourself on the back for sticking to the plan.

26 *Be Patient.* Blessings and curses can be confusing at times, but they are very present in our lives. Do not get easily discouraged or agitated when you have not seen any sign of success yet. Just keep a positive mindset, and learn all that you can about the industry that you are in. Over time, you will discover whether you belong and where you should be. Just have patience.

 27 ***Do Not Focus on the Closed Door when you stand Six Inches from an Open One.*** We tend to focus on the closed door, therefore failing to see the open door of opportunities. Staying positive is a good way to approaching situations by looking for solutions and being willing to ignore the negative side. The belief system is by far one of the most powerful tools one can have. If you believe there is a way out, your brain naturally will keep thinking and figure a way out. That brain is everybody's internal computer. It is always there and always accessible, so use it as often as you can! Finding solutions is easier than you think.

 28 ***FAKE IT until You MAKE IT.*** This means you may act in a certain way or have an illusion of your future self before it becomes a reality. We human beings are completely gullible — as soon as you are able to convince yourself that something is to be true, somehow it will become true.

em 29 *Value Others.* Everyone wants to feel valued, so praise others as much as you can. Thank the people who have helped you before and always return a favour.

em 30 ***Learn the ART of Creating Money and the ART of Spending Money.*** Living a full life is about creating and managing wealth wisely. Making a lot of money and not spending it is just too silly and pointless! This book shows you how to build wealth and how to share it. Enjoying your wealth by providing beyond the basic needs and by contributing to society will help you become a more fulfilled and happy person. Living well is what every human strives for, and you have to be deliberate and decisive to achieve that. Enjoy creating wealth, but please do not wait until you think you have enough to enjoy your wealth. Be generous and give back by donating.

🎵 **31** *Be Thrifty — Always Prepare for Rainy Days.* The economy and market change periodically outside of our control. Plus our business may suddenly face new competitions. Therefore, it is always wise to save money in case of emergency. You just never know what will happen next. It is very important to live within your means and have a back-up plan, if necessary.

🎵 **32** *Make Up Stories.* You can always re-frame your mind to make up new stories for your life. You can always decide what you want to focus on. The best is to rewrite your story to support your situation rather than to detract you from moving forward. You are the author, so write an interesting, compassionate and inspiring story for yourself. Remember, there is always more to write in the following chapters.

🎵 **33** *Be Yourself.* No one else in this world can be you better than you can be yourself. We are all created with a unique footprint which cannot be replicated nor emulated. Therefore, be the best you. Always be honest about who you are. Be authentic and be empathetic. People notice every expression and reaction of yours. They can sense if you are embarrassed or confident. Everyone likes truthfulness because there is only one story. Lies need more lies to cover up and before long, it becomes a mess. Onlookers embrace the true you more than you know. Be yourself.

Gem 34 ***Be in Close Proximity to People Who Can Help.*** Hanging around with people who are doing similar things is the best way to learn how to get what you want. If you want wealth, try your best to surround yourself with people who know how to create it. If you want to start a business, join entrepreneur clubs and groups to build your own business network.

Gem 35 ***Keep Getting Up.*** If you feel like you are getting beaten up in a boxing ring, get up and keep fighting. Do not give up. It is harder for your opponents to win if you just will not quit.

Gem 36 ***Be Your Own Biggest Fan.*** You are your own best cheerleader. Keep up the enthusiasm. Always encourage yourself. Keep going for the gold. Root for yourself because you know you are a winner!

Curtain Call:
My Standing Ovation to...

My Writing Team:

Thank you so much for assisting me in finishing this Masterpiece. Without you, this still would be a work in progress. I am eternally grateful for your deep friendship, guidance and contribution.

Editor,
Theme Designer and Graphic Artist:
Rod Chow - The one I can always depend on no matter what. You're the special person whom I count my blessings on every morning I wake up. I could not have done this without you. Thank you.

Content Editor:
Ellen Wong - No words can describe my gratitude for the countless hours of editing, rewriting and revising. Your persistence has helped me take this project to the finish line.

Publisher:

Bob Burnham & Dr. Paul Newton - My appreciation to you for all your professional guidance which has culminated in my now being able to proudly declare myself as a published author.

My Family:

The support and love you have given me through this journey is out of this world. I could not ask for a better family. You are the reasons for my existence and the anchor to all I do.

Rinco Chan - My soulmate and bestest friend. I "lobe" you!

Avery Chan- My one and only, you're the reason why I wrote this.

Mom - Thank you for teaching me leadership, philanthropy and humanity at such a young age.

Dad - Thank you for showing me the truly meaning of perseverance and to never, ever give up.

Winnie Chan - For always being my role model of success.

Ken Chan - For showing up whenever I needed support. Thank you from my heart.

Peter Cheung - The genius behind my business ideas, endeavours and accomplishments.

Rebecca Cheung - The best sis-in-law I can ever ask for and more...

Special thanks:

Nancy Leung	Erika Chan	Winnie Chan
Lamont Chan	Celin Cheung	Jayden Molero-Chan
Irene Tong	Janelle Cheung	

My Friends:

Thank you for your support and friendship throughout the years...

Mandy Lin	Eliza Ip	Esther Chiew
Thomas Ta	Kapo Chan	Beverly Yeung
Sam Chung	Alan Tam	Jessica Yeung
Jason Tam	Jacky Cheung	Denise Wong
Emily Vi	Gregory Rivers	Theresa Shaw
Darlene Tychansky	Hui Chi Sing	Daniel Langevin
Rob Lui	Khloe Chu	Karim Mohamedani
Jennifer Li	Kimman Wong	Michele Wong
Carol Lee	Joei So	Eric Ngo
Kent Lee	Sam Ho	Richmond Yu
Natalia Mak	May Soo	Jeinny Louie
Naomi Mak	Peter Poon	Ray Jivra
Gloria Fong	Kent Ling	Wendy Jivra
May Chan	Stephen Duke	Jeanette Lim
Ken Fong	Winnie Guo	

My Clients:

You have given me your confidence to be part of your journey. I am truly honored that you have embraced my direction, guidance and coaching. I am so endeared to see your dreams and wants come true. Thank you for letting me share your stories.

My Readers:

Thank you for enjoying my Composition. I hope that each of my Movements from I to X has **moved you** to take action to re-ignite your dreams and begin realizing them today. To me, my words are my music. It's been my pleasure to share my Concerto with you. I trust I have given you the confidence to live your true potential and put you on the road to success. I am privileged to impart my simple secrets to winning the money game to help you build an extraordinary life and create your life's masterpiece.

With love,

Wendy Yau Sum Cheung

Encore:
Contact My Team
to Sustain Your Applause

For more treasures, visit www.wendycheung.net

For further research on my business history, visit:

www.createyourlifesmasterpiece.com

www.altureproperties.com

www.mozartschool.com

www.simplymoneyinc.com

www.wendycheungteam.com

www.liveablife.com

www.magicalmusical.ca

My Contact Information

Phone: (604) 262-4836

info @createyourlifesmasterpiece.com

www.createyourlifesmasterpiece.com

IMPORTANT NOTE:

The stories in this book were shared with permission from all of my clients but each and every one of their names has been changed for the sake of their privacy.

DISCLAIMER NOTE:

Any results portrayed in this book are by no means an implied guarantee of individual outcomes. Individual performance vary according to the person's individual financial status and can be affected by many factors such as, but not limited to market conditions, lending rules and property location.

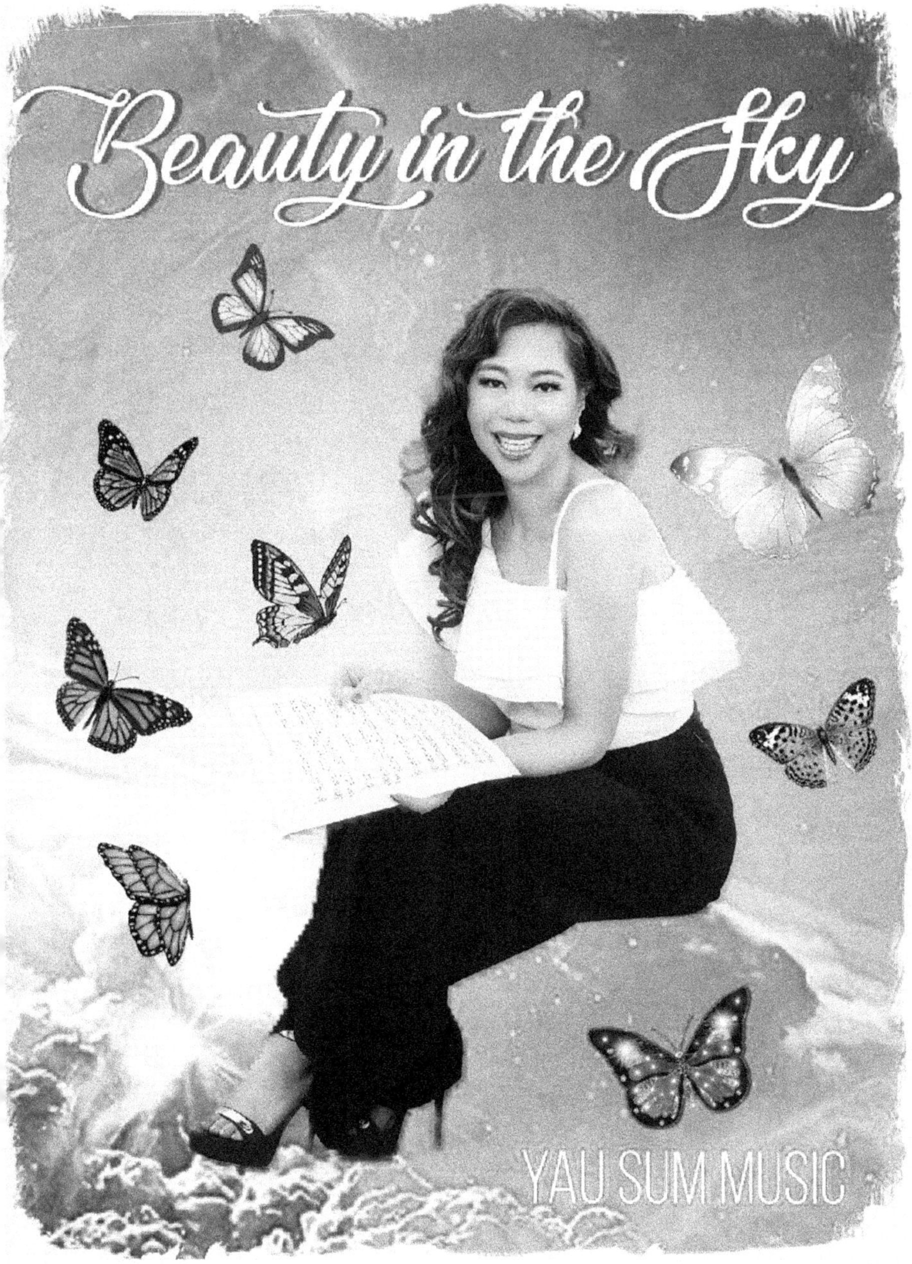
Beauty in the Sky
YAU SUM MUSIC

Create Your Life's Masterpiece

BEAUTY IN THE SKY

Words and Music by
Wendy Yau Sum Cheung

Expressively ♩ = 63

BEAUTY IN THE SKY

Yau Sum Music

Butterfly

I am so endeared and humbled to be able to express my musical passion with you in two original pieces of sheet music which I wrote specifically for this book.

My ballad, *Beauty in the Sky*, takes you on an emotional story of my life, and shares my inspiration for wanting to help you transform your life as well. It encapsulates how something so seemingly innocent, like a butterfly sticker in a corner store, could have such an impactful influence on one's journey.

Everything does happen for a reason, and the fact that you have my book in your hands may be the reason your life can take another path too, one that you passionately desire. I wish that each turn of the page will resonate with you, like the sound of beautiful music filling the air.

The Piano solo piece, *Butterfly*, is comprised of 4 bars of music placed atop of the title pages of each Movement in the book. "365" notes and "52" bars, which will follow you each day and every week throughout the year. In fact, if you play the 4 bars in order, you will have played the entire piece by the time you finish this book!

Butterfly's theme, an 8 note motif which appears in the header of every other page, represents the 8 Strategies of Profiting. This "jingle" is comprised of exactly 9 beats, representing the 9 Principles of Success. As well, there are a number of other serendipitous associations within this book which just happen to be, because again, everything does happen for a reason.

I designed and structured this book as my personal "Concerto" to you because I believe that music can mesmerize, inspire and emotionally engage, which can then lead you to find your inner peace and enlightenment.

So, I welcome those musically inclined to play and sing along, and for all of you to be immersed in this book. I hope it will bring to you true prosperity – love, wealth and a beautiful life – your own masterpiece to live.

Love,

Wendy Yau Sum Cheung

Butterfly

Solo Piano

Wendy Yau Sum Cheung

Moderately slow, expressively

Pedal ad lib. throughout

rit.

Butterfly

rit.

CPSIA information can be obtained
at www.ICGtesting.com
Printed in the USA
LVHW081322020920
664857LV00014B/142